NEVER GIVE UP ON HOPE

For there is hope of a tree, if it be cut down, that it will sprout again, and that the tender branch thereof will not cease.

Job 14:7

by

Franklin N. Abazie

Never Give Up On Hope
COPYRIGHT 2017 BY Franklin N Abazie
ISBN: 978-1-945-133-48-0

All right reserved. This book or any portion thereof may not be reproduced or used in any manner whatsoever without the express written permission of the publisher, except for the use of brief quotations in a book review. All Bible quotes are from King James Version and others as noted.

Published by: F N ABAZIE PUBLISHING HOUSE- aka, Empowerment Bookstore.

That I may publish with the voice of thanksgiving and tell of all thy wondrous works.
Psalms 26:7

To order additional copies, wholesales
or booking:
Call the Church office (973-372-7518),
or Empowerment Bookstore Hotline (973-393-8518)

Worship address:
343 Sanford Avenue Newark New Jersey 07106
Administrative Head Office address:
33 Schley Street Newark New Jersey 07112
Email:pastorfranknto@yahoo.com
Website www.fnabaziehealingministries.org
Publishing House: www.fnabaziepublishinghouse.org

This book is a production of F N Abazie Publishing House.
A publication Arms of Miracle of God Ministries 2017.
First Edition

CONTENTS

THE MANDATE OF THE COMMISSION iv
ARMS OF THE COMMISSION v
INTRODUCTION vii
CHAPTER 1
1 Why Do We Hope in God? 1
CHAPTER 2
2 The Reward of Hope in God 6
CHAPTER 3
3 Prayer of Salvation 49
CHAPTER 4
4 About The Author 58

THE MANDATE OF THE COMMISSION

"The moment is due to impact your world through the revival of the healing & miracle ministry of Jesus Christ of Nazareth."

"I am sending you to restore health unto thee and I will heal thee of thy wounds, said the Lord of Host."

ARMS OF THE COMMISSION

1) F N Abazie Ministries-Miracle of God Ministries (Miracle Chapel Intl)

2) F N Abazie TV Ministries: Global Television Ministry Outreach

3) F N Abazie Radio Ministries: Radio Broadcasting Outreach

4) F N Abazie Publishing House: Book Publication

5) F N Abazie Bible School: also called Word of Healing Bible School (W.O.H.B.S)

6) F N Abazie Evangelistic Ass: Miracle of God Ministries: Global Crusade

7) Empowerment Bookstore: Book distribution

8) F N Abazie Helping Hands: Meeting the help of the needy world wide

9) F N Abazie Disaster Recovery Mission: Global Disaster Recovery

10) F N Abazie Prison Ministry: Prison Ministry for all convicts "Second chance"

Some of our ministry arms are waiting the appointed time to commence.

FAVOR CONFESSION

Father thank you for making me righteous and accepted through the blood of Jesus Christ. Because of that, I am blessed and highly favored by God. I am the subject of your affection. Your favor surrounds me as a shield, and the first thing that people see around me is your favored shield.

Thank you that I have favor with you and man today. All day long people go out of their way to bless me and help me. I have favor with everyone that I deal with today. Doors that were once closed are now opened for me. I receive preferential treatment, and I have special privileges, I am Gods favored child.

No good thing will he withhold from me. Because of Gods favor my enemies cannot triumph over my life. I have supernatural increase and promotion. I declare restoration to everything that the devil has stolen from my life. I have honor in the midst of my adversaries and an increase in assets, especially in real estate and expansion of territories.

Because I am highly favored by God, I experience great victories, supernatural turnarounds, and miraculous breakthrough in the midst of great impossibilities. I receive recognition, prominence, and honor. Petitions are granted to me even by ungodly authorities. Policies, rules, regulations, and laws are changed and reverse on my behalf.

I win battles that I don't even have to fight, because God fights them for me. This is the day, the set time and the designated moment for me to experience the free favor of God, that profusely and lavishly abound on my behalf in Jesus name. **Amen.**

INTRODUCTION

"For to him that is joined to all the living there is hope: for a living dog is better than a dead lion." **Eccl 9:4**

This publication is a book of encouragement for anyone to hope and trust in the Lord Jesus. In my own opinion without *hope in God*, we will remain frustrated and in despair in life. The teachings in this publication will help anyone find *hope in God*. In this publication, it is my joy to uncover the mysteries *hope in God* in time of need.

In this book I have tried to emphasize about the reward of *hope in God*. Unless we remain calm in the midst of prevailing challenges, we will miss our glorious future. There is absolute power in positive people who believe and *hope in God. It is written*

"For there is hope of a tree, if it be cut down, that it will sprout again, and that the tender branch thereof will not cease."
Job 14:7

We must emancipate ourselves from mental slavery by building up inner strength, self-confidence, and faith in God. So many folks give up hope at the slightest temptation that comes their way. Others get frustrated, and fall into depression, just at the slightest challenge of life.

"Cast not away therefore your confidence, which hath great recompence of reward. For ye have need of patience, that, after ye have done the will of God, ye might

receive the promise." (Hebrew 10:35-36) My primary motive for this book, is to encourage you, never to give up *hope in God*. May the spiritual intention of this publication find expression upon your life in the mighty Name of Jesus. Amen.

HIS DESTINY WAS THE **CROSS....**

HIS PURPOSE WAS **LOVE.....**

HIS REASON WAS **YOU....**

"For there is hope of a tree, if it be cut down, that it will sprout again, and that the tender branch thereof will not cease."

Job 14:7

NEVER AGAIN PRAYER POINTS

"Hope deferred maketh the heart sick: but when the desire cometh, it is a tree of life.."
Proverb 13:12

I declare NEVER AGAIN! to any bad experience I have had in my life, it shall not repeat itself, in the name of Jesus.

I come against repeated oppression in the Name of Jesus.

I come against any family strong man, in the name of Jesus.

I destroy repeated calamities in the Mighty Name of Jesus.

AFFLICTION! Hear the word of the Lord, NEVER AGAIN will you rise!!! in the name of Jesus.

Witchcraft manipulations, NEVER AGAIN! in the name of Jesus.

Demonic powers assigned to use me as foot mat, I cry against you, NEVER AGAIN! in the name of Jesus.

The power behind 'almost there', I cry against you, NEVER AGAIN! in the name of Jesus.

Spirit of confusion, I cry against you, NEVER AGAIN! in the name of Jesus.

Powers closing my heavens, I cry against you, NEVER AGAIN! in the name of Jesus.

Spirit of stagnation, assigned against my life, I cry against you, NEVER AGAIN! in the name of Jesus.

Access of darkness into my life, TERMINATE BY FIRE! in the name of Jesus.

The lions of past problems roaring against me, SHUT UP! BE SILENCED!! in the name of Jesus.

Shame and disfavor, I cry against you, NEVER AGAIN! in the name of Jesus.

Diminishing returns, I cry against you, NEVER AGAIN! in the name of Jesus.

Visitations of the merchants of death, DIE!!! in the name of Jesus.

Satanic embarrassments, I cry against you, NEVER AGAIN! in the name of Jesus.

EVERYTHING, hear the word of the Lord, TURN AROUND FOR MY FAVOUR!!! in the name of Jesus.

I dismantle every strong hold designed to imprison my talent in the mighty name of Jesus.

I reject every cycle of frustration, in the name of Jesus.

Power of God paralyze every agent assigned to frustrate my life in the name of Jesus.

Finger of God, grant me supernatural speed against all my contenders in the name of Jesus.

By the blood of Jesus, I destroy every familiar spirit caging my life and career.

Fire of God arrest every demonic agents, assigned to police my destiny and marriage.

By the blood of Jesus, I proclaim no weapon fashioned against me shall ever prosper.

Holy Spirit of God break me through and forward in life in the mighty name of Jesus.

God, smash me and renew my strength, in the name of Jesus.

Holy Spirit, open my eyes to see beyond the visible to the invisible, in the name of Jesus.

Father Lord grant me strength and power in the name of Jesus.

O Lord, liberate my spirit to follow the leading of the Holy Spirit.

Holy Spirit, teach me to pray through problems instead of praying about, it in the name of Jesus.

Father Lord, deliver me from the false accusation in life, in the name of Jesus.

By the blood of Jesus, every evil spiritual padlock and evil chain hindering my success, be roasted, in the name of Jesus.

By the blood of Jesus I rebuke every spirit of spiritual deafness and blindness in my life, in the name of Jesus.

Father Lord, empower me to dominate the enemy of my destiny in the name of Jesus.

Jesus Christ of Nazareth, heal my infirmities in the name of Jesus.

Lord, anoint my eyes and my ears that they may see and hear wondrous things from heaven.

Father Lord, anoint me with power and authority to dominate all my enemies in the name of Jesus.

Fire of God roast every giant rising up against my life and career.

Holy Spirit of God destroy all my oppressors in the name of Jesus.

Angels of good new, bring my good news to me in the mighty name of Jesus.

Every strong man holding me down, lose your hold now in the name of Jesus.

I nullify every demonic prediction over my life in the name of Jesus.

By the blood of Jesus, I flush out every polluted deposit of the enemy in my life.

By the blood of Jesus, I paralyze every enemy of my promotion in the name of Jesus.

Father Lord, destroy any power tormenting my life that is not from you.

Holy Ghost fire, ignite the fire of revival in my life.

By the blood of Jesus, I declare victory over every conflicting trial.

By the Blood of Jesus, I command the arrest of every demonic spirit, militating against my life.

By the blood of Jesus, I proclaimed the blood of Jesus, over every device of the enemy.

By the blood of Jesus, I revoke stagnation and hardship over my life in the name of Jesus.

Holy Ghost fire, destroy every satanic arrangement in my life, in the name of Jesus.

YOU ARE THE PRODUCT OF YOUR THOUGHTS

It is written, *"For as he thinketh in his heart, so is he: Eat and drink, saith he to thee; but his heart is not with thee."* **Proverb 23:7**

Unless we understand the mystery of faith, we will lose hope, and miss out on God's blessings. Life is practical and not mystical. We are told *"And be not conformed to this world: but be ye transformed by the renewing of your mind, that ye may prove what is that good, and acceptable, and perfect, will of God."* (Romans 12:2)

We are absolutely responsible for the outcome of our thought. Our thoughts produce our words, our words define our action. With these patterns in mind, our actions define our habits, and our habits define our character, and our character becomes our lifestyle.

We must therefore believe in God and join our faith in God. *"For to him that is joined to all the living there is hope: for a living dog is better than a dead lion."* (Ecll 9:4) It is proven that you become the product of your thought.

"And be not conformed to this world: but be ye transformed by the renewing of your mind, that ye may prove what is that good, and acceptable, and perfect, will of God." (Romans 12:2)

What Does It Mean To Hope in God?

Often we claim to have *hope in God*, but the truth is most of us genuinely place hope in the governmental system. This government system will fail us any day, because it is designed by a man. We hope in our pension and 401k. We hope in the stock market and in the equity of our house. These things are material things that will rust and melt away. We often plan for retirement but we do not plan for eternity and for heaven.

Most people claim to love God but they cannot help out a stranger on the street. If you must find *hope in God*, we must change the way we think, the way we live, and the way we deal with everyone around us. *"For in him we live, and move, and have our being; as certain also of your own poets have said, For we are also his offspring."* (Acts 17:26)

It is written, "We know that we have passed from death unto life, because we love the brethren. He that loveth not his brother abideth in death. Whosoever hateth his brother is a murderer: and ye know that no murderer hath eternal life abiding in him.

Hereby perceive we the love of God, because he laid down his life for us: and we ought to lay down our lives for the brethren. But whoso hath this world's good, and seeth his brother have need, and shutteth up his bowels of compassion from him, how dwelleth the love of God in him? My little children, let us not love in word, neither in tongue; but in deed and in truth." **(1 John 3:14-18)**

To *hope in God* means to help out stranger and

people in need. We are told *"Withhold not good from them to whom it is due, when it is in the power of thine hand to do it."* **(Proverb 3:27)**

To hope in God means to be willing to entertain stranger. It is written *"Be not forgetful to entertain strangers: for thereby some have entertained angels unawares."* **(Hebrews 13:2)** Remember… *"Therefore to him that knoweth to do good, and doeth it not, to him it is sin."* **(James 4:17)**

To *hope in God*, we must not have any other alternative in life. *"My soul, wait thou only upon God; for my expectation is from him."* (Psalms 62:5) We must put our trust and hope in God. *"In God I will praise his word, in God I have put my trust; I will not fear what flesh can do unto me."* (Psalm 56:4)

"He delighteth not in the strength of the horse: he taketh not pleasure in the legs of a man. The Lord taketh pleasure in them that fear him, in those that hope in his mercy." (Psalms 147:10-11)

It is written...

"Trust in the Lord with all thine heart; and lean not unto thine own understanding. In all thy ways acknowledge him, and he shall direct thy paths." (Proverb 3:5-6)

Remember…

"And they that know thy name will put their trust in thee: for thou, Lord, hast not forsaken them that seek thee."

(Psalms 9:10) We must all hope in God and never give up in life. One man said that failure is an opportunity to begin again in life. I define failure as

F—First

A—Attempt

I—In

L—Learning

A practical example of a man who never gave on hope, worked his way up to become the president of the United States of America. The story of Abraham Lincoln is a typical story that reflects the title of this book.

Abraham Lincoln was an American politician and lawyer who served as the 16th President of the United States from March 1861 until his assassination in April 1865. Abraham Lincoln *"Never gave up on hope."* This is a ubiquitous piece of American historical glurge that has been printed in countless magazines and newspaper columns over the decades, including an appearance in a 1967 Reader's Digest collection of humor and anecdotes. It is now a favorite feature of inspirational e-mail lists, websites, and Chicken Soup for the Soul-type books, and it exemplifies what is so very wrong about turning history into glurge.

Abraham Lincoln is the mythical, towering figure of American history, and whatever one thinks of his accomplishments, he was indeed a fascinating character. He truly fulfilled the title of this small book "never give up on hope." He was the man with almost no education, born in a one-room log cabin, honest and hard-working, who overcame numerous challenges, and failures, in life to become President of the United States when the nation was confronted with its bloodiest predicament.

One would think the facts of Lincoln's life should be a good enough story for anyone, but no, apparently the truth isn't sufficiently inspirational; it has to be shaped and molded into glurge that depicts Lincoln as a man who endured repeated failures, and defeats from the time he was born until he was elected President of USA. Lincoln certainly survived his fair share of hardship and setbacks, but he also *never gave up on hope* throughout his lifetime. In my opinion, *if you can endure the cross, you will wear the crown. Know this today, winners never win. And those who quit never win in life. I see you coming out of your present predicament in Jesus Name.*

A brief history below supports my case that Abraham Lincoln *never gave up on hope. I pray in the Name of Jesus Christ, that you too will never give on hope in your life.*

1816: His family was forced out of their home. He had to work to support them.

Life on the American frontier in the early 19th century was no picnic for anyone; it required hours of back-breaking toil and drudgery day in and day out. In the context of their time, however, the Lincolns lived under rather unremarkable circumstances.

The statement that the Lincolns were "forced out of their home" in 1816 isn't completely false, but it is somewhat misleading because it implies they were suddenly and involuntarily uprooted from their home, with no warning and no place to go. Abraham Lincoln's father, Thomas, had owned farmland in Hardin County, Kentucky, since the early 1800s, and he left Kentucky and moved his family across the Ohio River to Indiana in 1816 for two primary reasons:

Kentucky was a slave state, and Thomas Lincoln disliked slavery — both because his church opposed it, and because he did not want to have to compete economically with slave labor.

Kentucky had never been properly surveyed, and many settlers in the early 1800s found that establishing clear title to their land was difficult. Thomas Lincoln (and other farmers in the area) were eventually sued by non-Kentucky residents who claimed prior title to their lands.

With plenty of lands available in neighboring Indiana, a territory where slavery had been excluded by the Northwest Ordinance and the government guaranteed buyers clear title to their property, Thomas Lincoln opted to move rather than to spend time and money fighting over the title to his Kentucky farm. So, in a moderate sense the Lincolns could be said to have been "forced out of their home," but it did not happen abruptly, and they opted to leave because better opportunities awaited them.

The other part of this statement, that a seven-year-old Abraham Lincoln "had to work to support" his family, is also misleading. Young Abraham did not have to take an outside job lest his poor family sink into financial ruin. Like nearly all farm children of his era, Lincoln was expected to perform whatever chores and tasks he was physically capable of handling around the farm. If Abraham worked harder and longer than most other children, it was not because the Lincolns' circumstances were extraordinarily difficult, but because Lincoln was exceptionally tall and strong for his age.

1818: His mother died.

This, at least, is no embellishment. Lincoln's mother, Nancy, did die of "milk sickness" in 1818, when Abraham was only nine years old. A mother's death is a tragedy for any child, and it was a special hardship for a struggling farm family.

1831: Failed in business.

The statement that Lincoln "failed in business" in 1831 is another misleading claim, because it implies that he was the owner or operator of the failed business, or at least was otherwise responsible for its failure. None of this is true. Lincoln left his father's home for good in 1831 and, along with his cousin John Hanks, took a flatboat full of provisions down the Mississippi River from Illinois to New Orleans on behalf of a "bustling, none too scrupulous businessman" named Denton Offutt. Offutt planned to open a general store, and he promised to make Lincoln its manager when Abraham returned from New Orleans. Lincoln operated the store as Offutt's clerk and assistant for several months (and by all accounts did a fine job of it) until Offutt, a poor businessman, overextended himself financially and ran it into the ground. Thus by the spring of 1832 Lincoln had indeed "lost his job," but not because he had "failed in business."

1832: Ran for state legislature – lost.

Lincoln did run for the Illinois state legislature in 1832, although as Lincoln biographer David Herbert Donald noted, "the post he was seeking was not an elevated one … [legislators] dealt mostly with such issues as whether cattle had to be fenced in or could enjoy free range." Lincoln finished eighth in a field of thirteen (with the top four vote-getters becoming legislators). However, this same year Lincoln also achieved something of which he was very proud, when the members of a volunteer militia company he had joined selected him as their captain. Lincoln said many years later that this was "a success which gave me more pleasure than any I have had since." (He also noted later in his career that his defeat in the 1832 legislative election was the only time he "was ever beaten on a direct vote of the people.")

1832: Also lost his job – wanted to go to law school but couldn't get in.

As noted above, Lincoln actually "lost his job" in 1831, and the notion that in 1832 Lincoln "wanted to go to law school but couldn't get in" (why he couldn't get in remains unspecified) is both inaccurate and an anachronism. Lincoln did eventually become a lawyer, and he accomplished the feat in the manner typical of his time and place: not by attending law school, but by reading law books and observing court sessions. He was indeed interested in becoming a lawyer as early as 1832, but, as Lincoln biographer Donald wrote, "on reflection he concluded that he needed a better education to succeed."

1833: Borrowed some money from a friend to begin a business and by the end of the year he was bankrupt. He spent the next 17 years of his life paying off this debt.

Lincoln and William F. Berry, a corporal from Lincoln's militia company, purchased a general store in New Salem, Illinois, in 1833. (Lincoln had no money for his half; he didn't technically "borrow the money from a friend" but instead signed a note with one of the previous owners for his share.) Lincoln and Berry were competing against a larger, well-organized store in the same town; their outfit did little business, and within a short time it had "winked out."

The debt on the store became due the following year, and since Lincoln was unable to pay off his note, his possessions were seized by the sheriff. Moreover, when Lincoln's former partner died with no assets soon afterwards, Lincoln insisted upon assuming his partner's half of the debt as well, even though he was not legally obligated to do so. Exactly how long it took Lincoln to pay off this debt (which he jokingly referred to as his "national debt") in its entirety is unknown. It did take him several years, but not seventeen; nor, as this statement implies, was he completely financially encumbered until it was paid in full. Within a few months of the store's failure Lincoln had obtained a position as the New Salem postmaster, and by 1835 he was earning money both as a surveyor and as a state legislator.

1834: Ran for state legislature again – won.

In 1834 Lincoln was again one of thirteen candidates running for a seat in the state legislature, and this time he won, securing the second-highest vote total among the field.

1835: Was engaged to be married, sweetheart died and his heart was broken.

Much of Lincoln's relationship with New Salem resident Ann Rutledge remains a mystery, and several aspects of it — including whether or not they were actually engaged (at the time they met, Ann was betrothed to someone else) — are based more on speculation than documented fact. Whatever the exact nature of their relationship, however, her death in the summer of 1835 appears to have affected Lincoln profoundly.

1836: Had a total nervous breakdown and was in bed for six months.

Whether Lincoln experienced a "total nervous breakdown" in the aftermath of Ann Rutledge's death is debatable, but the notion that he somehow found time to stay "in bed for six months" is not. After Ann's funeral he spent a few weeks visiting an old friend, and within a month of her death he had resumed his occasional surveying duties. He surveyed the nearby town of Petersburg in February 1836, undertook a strenuous two-month campaign for re-election during the summer, and served in the state legislature throughout the year. All of this would have been difficult for a man who spent "six months in bed."

1838: Sought to become speaker of the state legislature – defeated.

By the time of the 1838-39 legislative session, Lincoln had twice been an unsuccessful Whig candidate for the position of speaker of the Illinois House of Representatives. This was a relatively minor political setback, however, and no mention is made here of the fact that by 1838 he was one of the most experienced members of the legislature, or of any of the other notable successes he achieved between 1834 and 1838, namely:

He was re-elected to the state legislature in 1836 and 1838, both times receiving more votes than any other candidate. The Illinois Supreme Court licensed him to practice law in 1837.

He became the partner of "one of the most prominent and successful lawyers in Springfield" (where he now lived).

1840: Sought to become elector – defeated.

This statement is erroneous. Lincoln was named as a presidential elector at the Illinois state Whig convention on 8 October 1839, and he campaigned as a Whig elector during the 1840, 1844, 1852, and 1856 presidential elections (skipping the 1848 campaign because he was serving in Congress.)

1843: Ran for Congress – lost.

One could claim this as a Lincoln failure in that he wanted to be a Congressman and failed to achieve that goal, but it is technically inaccurate to claim that he "ran for Congress" in 1843 and lost: The election was held in 1844, and Lincoln was not a candidate in that election. Lincoln's failure to achieve his party's nomination at the May 1843 Whig district convention is undoubtedly what is referred to here.

1846: Ran for Congress again – this time he won – went to Washington and did a good job.

Lincoln won a seat as an Illinois representative to the U.S. Congress in 1846.

1848: Ran for re-election to Congress – lost.

Lincoln did not "lose" the 1848 election. He did not run for re-election because Whig policy at the time specified that party members should step aside after serving one term to allow other members to take their turns at holding office. Lincoln, a faithful party member, complied.

1849: Sought the job of land officer in his home state – rejected.

The position referred to here was commissioner of the General Land Office, a federal position, not a state one, and one that came with a fair amount of power and patronage. Since Lincoln's term in Congress was about to expire, his friends urged him to apply for this post, but Lincoln was reluctant to give up his law career. He finally agreed to apply for the job when the choice was deadlocked between two other Illinois candidates and it looked like the appointment might, therefore, go to a compromise candidate from outside of Illinois. Whigs from northern Illinois then decided that too many appointments were going to party members from other parts of the state and put up their own candidate against Lincoln. The choice was left to the Secretary of the Interior, who selected the other candidate.

1854: Ran for Senate of the United States – lost.

In Lincoln's time, U.S. senators were not elected through direct popular vote; they were appointed by state legislatures. In Illinois, voters cast ballots only for state legislators, and the General Assembly of the state legislature then selected nominees to fill open U.S. Senate seats. So, in 1854 (and again in 1856) Lincoln was not technically running for the Senate; he was campaigning on behalf of Whig candidates for state legislature seats all throughout Illinois. Nonetheless, after the 1854 state election, Lincoln made it known that he sought the open U.S. Senate seat for Illinois. The first ballot of a divided General Assembly was taken in February 1855, and Lincoln received the most votes but was six votes shy of the requisite majority. When the process remained deadlocked after another eight ballots, Lincoln withdrew from the race to lend his support to another candidate and ensure that the Senate seat did not go to a pro-slavery Democrat.

1856: Sought the Vice-Presidential nomination at his party's national convention – got less than 100 votes.

This is both misleading and inaccurate. Lincoln did not "seek" the vice-presidential nomination at the 1856 Republican national convention in Philadelphia; his name was put into nomination by the Illinois delegation after most national delegates were already committed to other candidates. (Lincoln himself was back in Illinois, not at the convention, and did not know he had been nominated until friends brought him the news.) Nonetheless, in an informal ballot, Lincoln received 110 votes out of 363, not at all a bad showing for someone who was little known outside his home state.

1858: Ran for U.S. Senate again – again he lost.

Again, Lincoln was not directly campaigning for a Senate seat, although it was a foregone conclusion that he would be the Republicans' choice to take Stephen Douglas' U.S. Senate seat if his party won control of the Illinois state legislature. Lincoln actually bested Douglas in the sense that Republican legislative candidates statewide received slightly over 50% of the popular vote, but the Republicans failed to gain control of the state legislature, and Douglas, therefore, retained his seat in the Senate.

1860: Elected president of the United States.

I pray you never give up on hope in your lifetime. Abraham lincoln on Tuesday, Nov 8th 1864 won reelection for the president of USA. what a life story. "NEVER GIVE UP ON HOPE"

CHAPTER 1

WHY DO WE HOPE IN GOD?

"For to him that is joined to all the living there is hope: for a living dog is better than a dead lion." **Eccl 9:4**

In one simple sentence. We should *"hope in God"* because God is the giver of life, the source of our existence and the bridge of hope for every believer alive. Although hope is a doing word, it is a verb which also means: to desire with expectation of obtainment; to expect with confidence. We are told by the Holy Scripture that *"Hope deferred maketh the heart sick: but when the desire cometh, it is a tree of life."* (Proverb 13:12)

Unless we develop genuine love for God, and the Kingdom of God (the church), and for others around us, we will forever live in frustration. *"Every time you live for others, you live forever, but when you live to yourself, you are reduced to self."* So many young Christians do not understand that hope is the catalyst for our salvation. It is written *"For we are saved by hope: but hope that is seen is not hope: for what a man seeth, why doth he yet hope for? But if we hope for that we see not, then do we with patience wait for it."* (Romans 8:24-25).

It is written *"who against hope believed in hope, that he might become the father of many nations, according to that which was spoken, So shall thy seed be."* **Romans 4:18**

Chapter 1 Why Do We Hope In God

Hope in the Lord gives us strength. The American culture teaches us to have self-confidence, but as believers, we are to place our confidence in the Lord. *"My soul, wait thou only upon God; for my expectation is from him."* (Psalm 62:5) Hope in God, grants us inner strength to confront prevailing challenges of life. David said *"In God have I put my trust: I will not be afraid what man can do unto me."* (Psalm 56:10). Every time we *hope in God* we develop inner strength and courage to face the most difficulty situations in life. It is believed that *hope in God* trains us to be people of endurance and patience.

Quiet often most of us forget to put our burden in to the hand of the Lord. When trouble comes our way we must always seek the face of the Lord in prayer, in supplications and in thanksgiving in life. *"Cast thy burden upon the Lord, and he shall sustain thee: he shall never suffer the righteous to be moved."* (Psalms 55:22)

Whenever we are confronted with frustrating challenges in life, we must return to God in prayers with a humble heart and with patient. The attitude of prayer is the key to overcome anxiety and the worries of life. We secure God's protection and discovers inner peace in God's unconditional love for us. *Hope in God* grants strength and encouragement. Jesus said *"Let not your heart be troubled: ye believe in God, believe also in me. In my Father's house are many mansions: if it were not so, I would have told you. I go to prepare a place for you."* (John 14:2)

Why Should We Hope In God?

I will give you a few examples. We should hope in God because of His great promises to us. *"But as it is written, Eye hath not seen, nor ear heard, neither have entered into the heart of man, the things which God hath prepared for them that love him."*
(1 Cor 2:9)

"According as his divine power hath given unto us all things that pertain unto life and godliness, through the knowledge of him that hath called us to glory and virtue: Whereby are given unto us exceeding great and precious promises: that by these ye might be partakers of the divine nature, having escaped the corruption that is in the world through lust." (2 Peter 1:3-4) To *hope in God* is among our primary responsibilities as believers.

Although most of us claim to be saved and righteous in life. Unless our heart is pure from any root of bitterness, and immorality, our salvation remains questionable. It is inevitable to genuinely *hope in God* with a defiled conscience. *Hope in God* is a catalyst that increases our expectation from God. *Hope in God* is medicinal, it helps our health, and increases our self-worth, confidence, and optimism. *"Why art thou cast down, O my soul? and why art thou disquieted within me? hope in God: for I shall yet praise him, who is the health of my countenance, and my God."* (Psalms 43:5)

It is proven with studies, that hopeful people have a stronger will – power and the tendency to overcome prevailing difficult situation in life. If you must *hope in God* you must know Him more in prayers, in supplication and in thanksgiving. As we spend time every day worshipping Him for His all sovereign power and greatness. *Hope in God* reminds us that we are never alone in this race of life. *"What shall we then say to these things? If God be for us, who can be against us?"* (Romans 8:31)

It is written...

"I wait for the Lord, my soul doth wait, and in his word do I hope. My soul waiteth for the Lord more than they that watch for the morning: I say, more than they that watch for the morning. Let Israel hope in the Lord: for with the Lord there is mercy, and with him is plenteous redemption." (Psalm 130:5-7)

We must realize this truth today about God. Every time we call for help in prayers, intercession, and thanksgiving, God intervenes for us quickly in life.

Hope in God secures mercy for us as believers

It is written *"He delighteth not in the strength of the horse: he taketh not pleasure in the legs of a man. The Lord taketh pleasure in them that fear him, in those that hope in his mercy."* (Psalms 147:10-11)

I pray, we will continue to hope in God. Regardless of the prevailing circumstances surrounding us, we will never give up on God. David said *"I will lift up mine eyes unto the hills, from whence cometh my help. My help cometh from the Lord, which made heaven and earth."* (Psalms 121:1-2)

May this psalms below become your prayer in the Name of Jesus.

"Out of the depths have I cried unto thee, O Lord. Lord, hear my voice: let thine ears be attentive to the voice of my supplications.
If thou, Lord, shouldest mark iniquities, O Lord, who shall stand?
But there is forgiveness with thee, that thou mayest be feared.
I wait for the Lord, my soul doth wait, and in his word do I hope.
My soul waiteth for the Lord more than they that watch for the morning:
I say, more than they that watch for the morning. Let Israel hope in the Lord:
for with the Lord there is mercy, and with him is plenteous redemption.
And he shall redeem Israel from all his iniquities." Psalms 130:1-8

CHAPTER 2

THE REWARD OF HOPE IN GOD

"Hope deferred maketh the heart sick: but when the desire cometh, it is a tree of life."
Proverb 13:12

Often most people think hope is an emotion. "I am feeling hopeful tonight," perhaps someone may say, but that is not correct of "hope". Hope means a determination to make God's promise concerning our life real and genuine. This I mean to believe in God's promise without reservation. To make God's word the final commandment over our life. To remain faithful even in the face of prevailing predicament.

Understand what we are saying. God will never reward anyone the same way our fellow men rewards us in life. Some church folks think that God will reward them directly from a particular source they sowed into. God will reward us according to His will. God will not reward us according to our desired expectation of Him. To hope in God by definition is a mystery of the covenant.

Every time we genuinely *hope in God* we provoke the mystery behind *hope in God* to validate itself. For God cannot deny Himself. In my own understanding *hope in God's* word grants us confidence and assurance. It is written *"Cast not away therefore your confidence, which hath great recompence of reward. For ye have need of patience, that, after ye have done the will of God, ye might receive the promise."* **(Hebrews 10:35-36)**

The key to overcome any prevailing challenge in life is to *hope in God. For we are saved by hope: but hope that is seen is not hope: for what a man seeth, why doth he yet hope for? But if we hope for that we see not, then do we with patience wait for it.* (Romans 8:24-25)

"For I know the thoughts that I think toward you, saith the Lord, thoughts of peace, and not of evil, to give you an expected end." (Jeremiah 29:11)

----Hope gives us something to look forward for

Hope in God grants us confidence and courage by raising our expectation, and self-confidence. This helps our mental and emotional wellbeing. *"And he gave heed unto them, expecting to receive something of them."* (Acts 3:5) We are told *"For the earnest expectation of the creature waiteth for the manifestation of the sons of God."* (Romans 8:19)

----Hope grants us confidence and assurance

If you are at a bus stop waiting for your next bus, unless you know when your bus is coming, you will never have rest of mind. Hope grants us the confidence to know when God's angels is on the way to deliver our blessing package. *"Cast not away therefore your confidence, which hath great recompence of reward. For ye have need of patience, that, after ye have done the will of God, ye might receive the promise."* (Hebrews 10:35-36).

----Hope keeps us alive

Without hope in the Lord, I tell you a lot of people would have committed suicide and died. There are so many depressed people. Most of these people are alive today by the mercy of God. It is written *"For to him that is joined to all the living there is hope: for a living dog is better than a dead lion."* (Eccl 9:4)

----Hope in God grants us relief and restoration in life

The life of Job is a typical example of ultimate restoration of hope for us all to emulate in life. It is recorded that despite Job's wife mockery to curse God and die, in chapter two verse nine. And despite losing all his properties, cattles, and business, yet, Job trusted in the Lord His God. Job made these outstanding remarkable statements. *And said, Naked came I out of my mother's womb, and naked shall I return thither: the Lord gave, and the Lord hath taken away; blessed be the name of the Lord."* (Job 1:21)

Job said

"Though he slay me, yet will I trust in him: but I will maintain mine own ways before him." (Job 13:15)

"For I know that my redeemer liveth, and that he shall stand at the latter day upon the earth" (Job 19:25)

God restored the life and wealth of Job because he trusted in Him. *"So the Lord blessed the latter end of Job more than his beginning: for he had fourteen thousand sheep, and six thousand camels, and a thousand yoke of oxen, and a thousand she asses."* (Job 42:12)

----God takes please whenever He finds us Hopeful

Whenever we prove our faithfulness to God, through our faith, hope, and love, God is obligated to reward us with supernatural breakthroughs, total restoration, and special promotions in life. It is written *"He delighteth not in the strength of the horse: he taketh not pleasure in the legs of a man. The Lord taketh pleasure in them that fear him, in those that hope in his mercy."* (Psalms 147:11-12)

----Hope grants us joy and peace in believing

It is written *"Now the God of hope fill you with all joy and peace in believing, that ye may abound in hope, through the power of the Holy Ghost."* (Romans 15:13)

Hope in God strengths both our belief system and our psyche. To *hope in God* means to mean whatever you say. We must make our confessed word to be in compliance with our actions in life. Our life must reflect what we believe, think, and confess in faith.

HINDERANCES TO HOPE IN GOD

~DESPERATION

Anytime you are in a hurry in life, you disqualify yourself from the blessings of God. Desperation hinders the mystery of *hope in God* from manifestation. Most folks say, I hope in God but they are in a rush and cannot wait for anything good to happen for them. It is written *"he that believeth shall not make haste."* (Isaiah 28:16)

We are certain to miss out on our blessing every time we are in a rush and desperate in life. Have you forgotten? *"Do not be anxious about anything, but in every situation, by prayer and petition, with thanksgiving, present your requests to God."* (Phil 4:6). In my own opinion, desperation proves that we lack faith in God. If we must hope in God, we must not be desperate. If faith in God must work for us, we must not be in a hurry in life.

~COVETOUSNESS

It's difficult to admit to greediness, but most of us are greedy to a high degree. God hates greedy people. We are told "And he said unto them, Take heed, and beware of covetousness: for a man's life consisteth not in the abundance of the things which he possesseth." (Luke

12:15) Most greedy people build their faith in fake hope. The truth is they build their hope in material things which has no genuine value in life. Recall.. "But godliness with contentment is great gain"

It is written *"Lay not up for yourselves treasures upon earth, where moth and rust doth corrupt, and where thieves break through and steal: But lay up for yourselves treasures in heaven, where neither moth nor rust doth corrupt, and where thieves do not break through nor steal:"* (Matthew 6:19-20)

~SIN IN OUR LIFE

Unless we deal with the old man of sin. We will never see true light in Christ. Unless we deal with sin in our lives, we will never experience genuine salvation in Christ. We are told "Wherefore he saith, Awake thou that sleepest, and arise from the dead, and Christ shall give thee light." (Ephesians 5:14).

Unless we are pure before Him, our hope in Him is fake. It is written, *"Blessed are the pure in heart: for they shall see God."* (Matthew 5:8) Unless we genuinely deal with sin in our lives, our *hope in God* is fake. We are told, *"Now we know that God heareth not sinners: but if any man be a worshipper of God, and doeth his will, him he heareth."*

Sin erodes destiny. It decays our glorious path. Remember...the path of a just man is like a shining light.." Proverb 4:18 *"If we confess our sins, he is faithful and just to forgive us our sins, and to cleanse us from all unrighteousness."* (1 John 1:9) Sin is among of the strongest forces that will stop anyone from entering the Kingdom of God in Heaven.

~PRIDE

Although they claim to *hope in God*, but most proud men/women do not genuinely *hope in God*. We are told that *God hates a proud look, a lying tongue, and hands that shed innocent blood.* If we claim to *hope in God* we must humble ourselves before him. Eventually, God will exalt us in due time. *"Humble yourselves therefore under the mighty hand of God, that he may exalt you in due time:"* (1 Peter 5:6) Pride hinder *hope in God. Pride goeth before destruction, and an haughty spirit before a fall.* (Proverb 16:18)

ACCESS INTO THE SUPERNATURAL

WALKING IN THE SPIRIT:

Unless we obey scriptural command we shall never operate in the supernatural. Every time we walk in the spirit we cheaply have access into the supernatural realm. In my opinion walking in the Spirit is the gateway into riches and abundance of wealth in Christ Jesus. *"But the natural man receiveth not the things of the Spirit of God: for they are foolishness unto him: neither can he know them, because they are spiritually discerned."* (1 Cor 2:14)

Remember…

"This I say then, Walk in the Spirit, and ye shall not fulfil the lust of the flesh." Gal 5:17

BORN AGAIN

However it may sound, we must hear it again. We must be born again. *"But the natural man receiveth not the things of the Spirit of God: for they are foolishness unto him: neither can he know them, because they are spiritually discerned."* If you are not born again, you are missing out on the blessings of God. For us to access the blessings of the Lord, we must genuinely repent of our sins. *"Jesus answered and said unto him, Verily, verily, I say unto thee, Except a man be born again, he cannot see the kingdom of God."* (John 3:3)

Born again status grants us access to unlimited riches of His glory. We must make plans to make heaven if we are genuinely serving God. Eternity is real make your own plan to make heaven by being born again.

FAITH

Faith in God is the platform to operate in the supernatural. Faith in God is the gateway for His unlimited riches. Faith in God is the breathing grounds for hope in God to manifest. Unless there is faith in God our hope is fake. *"For we are saved by hope: but hope that is seen is not hope: for what a man seeth, why doth he yet hope for?"* (Romans 8:24)

For anyone to access the supernatural we must

have genuine faith in God and in His word.
"And Jesus answering saith unto them, Have faith in God." (Mark 11:22). *"We having the same spirit of faith, according as it is written, I believed, and therefore have I spoken; we also believe, and therefore speak."* 2 Cor 4:13

WALK IN AGREEMENT

It is commanded to walk in agreement with the Holy Spirit. It is the will of God to walk according to the leading of the Holy Spirit. For no man can walk with God and fail in life. *"Can two walk together, except they both agreed?"* (Amos 3:3). For us to experience great things in life we must walk in agreement and in the spirit.

WALK IN LOVE

It is written *"but faith which worketh by love."* Walking in love grants us access into the deep things of God. We are told *"But as it is written, Eye hath not seen, nor ear heard, neither have entered into the heart of man, the things which God hath prepared for them that love him."* (1 Cor 2:9)

Walking in love grants us the unlimited access into His glory. *"And we have known and believed the love that God hath to us. God is love; and he that dwelleth in love dwelleth in God, and God in him."* (1 John 4:16)

WALK IN TRUTH

Most people, lie to their friends, to themselves, and to God, but until we tell ourselves the truth, we are not ready to walk into the miraculous in life. Walking in the truth, is the access key into signs and wonders. For unless we tell ourselves the truth we are not ready to experience the power of His majesty. We are told, *"For we can do nothing against the truth, but for the truth."* (2 Cor 13:8)

Unless we receive and believe the truth of God's word into our life, we will forever remain in want of all things. We must accept the truth and release ourselves from the shackles of deceit, fraud, malice, envy, strive, fornication adultery e.t.c. *"If the Son therefore shall make you free, ye shall be free indeed."* **John 8:32**

PRAYER POINTS THAT WORKS

I cancel my name and that of my family from the death register, with the fire of God, in the name of Jesus.

Every weapon of destruction fashioned against me and my family, be destroyed by the fire of God, in the name of Jesus.

Power of God, fight for me in every area of my life, in Jesus' name.

Every hindrance to my breakthrough, be melted by the fire of God, in the name of Jesus.

Every evil power against me, be scattered by the thunder fire of God, in the name of Jesus.

Father Lord, destroy every evil man/woman in the name of Jesus.

Every failures of the past, be converted to success , in Jesus' name.

Father Lord, let the former rain, the latter rain and Your blessing pour down on me now.

Father Lord, let all the failure turn into success for me, in the name of Jesus.

I receive power from on high and I paralyze all the powers of darkness that are diverting my blessings, in the name of Jesus.

Beginning from this day, I employ the services of the angels of God to open unto me every door of opportunity and breakthroughs, in the name of Jesus.

I will not go around in circles again, I will make progress, in the name of Jesus.

I shall not build for another to inhabit and I shall not plant for another to eat, in the name of Jesus.

I paralyse the powers of the emptier concerning my handywork, in the name of Jesus.

O Lord, let every locust, caterpillar and palmer-worm assigned to eat the fruit of my labour be roasted by the fire of God.

The enemy shall not spoil my testimony in this programme, in the name of Jesus.

By the blood of Jesus, I reject every backward journey, in the name of Jesus.

By the blood of Jesus, I paralyze every strongman attached to any area of my life, in the name of Jesus.

I pray, Let every agent of shame fashioned to work against my life be paralyzed, in the name of Jesus.

I paralyse the activities of household wickedness over my life, in the name of Jesus.

I quench every strange fire emanating from evil tongues against me, in the name of Jesus.

Father Lord, give me power for maximum achievement.

Heavenly father, give me comforting authority to achieve my goal.

Blood of Jesus Christ, defend and fortify me with Your power.

I paralyse every spirit of disobedience in my life, in Jesus' name.

I refuse to disobey the voice of God, in the name of Jesus.

Every root of rebellion in my life, be uprooted, in Jesus' name.

By the blood of Jesus, I destroy every witchcraft spirit in my life, in the name of Jesus.

Contradicting forces promoting hindrance in my life, die, in Jesus' name.

Blood of Jesus, blot out every evil mark of witchcraft in my life, in the name of Jesus.

Every garment put upon me by witchcraft, be torn to pieces, in the name of Jesus.

Angels of God, begin to pursue my household enemies, let their ways be dark and slippery, in the name of Jesus.

Lord, confuse them and turn them against themselves.

By the blood of Jesus, I break every evil unconscious agreement with household enemies concerning my miracles, in the name of Jesus.

Household witchcraft, fall down and die, in the name of Jesus.

Father Lord, drag all the household wickedness to the Dead Sea and bury them there.

Father Lord, I reject to follow the evil pattern of remote control my household enemies.

My life, jump out from the cage of household wickedness, in the name of Jesus.

I command all my blessings and potentials buried by wicked household enemies to be exhumed, in the name of Jesus.

I will see the goodness of the Lord in the land of the living, in the name of Jesus.

Everything done against me to spoil my joy, receive destruction, in the name of Jesus.

Father Lord, as Abraham received favor in Your eyes, let me receive Your favor, so that I can excel in every area of my life.

Lord Jesus, help my shortcoming and infirmities in the name of Jesus.

It does not matter, whether I deserve it or not, I receive immeasurable favor from the Lord, in the name of Jesus.

By the blood of Jesus I receive every blessing God has apportioned to me in the name of Jesus.

My blessing will not be transferred to my neighbor in the name of Jesus.

Father Lord, disgrace every power that is tormenting my breakthrough in the name of Jesus.

Every step I take shall lead to outstanding success, in Jesus' name.

I shall prevail with man and with God in every area of my life, in the name of Jesus.

Every habitation of infirmity in my life, break to pieces, in the name of Jesus.

My body, soul and spirit, reject every evil load, in Jesus' name.

Evil foundation in my life, I pull you down today, in the mighty name of Jesus.

Every inherited sickness in my life, depart from me now, in the name of Jesus.

Every evil water in my body, get out, in the name of Jesus.

By the blood of Jesus, I cancel the effect of every evil dedication in my life, in the name of Jesus.

Holy Ghost fire, immunize my blood against satanic poisoning, in the name of Jesus.

Father Lord, put self control in my mouth, in the name of Jesus.

I refuse to get accustomed to sickness, in the name of Jesus.

Every door open to infirmity in my life, be permanently closed today, in the name of Jesus.

Every power contenting with God in my life, be roasted, in the name of Jesus.

Every power preventing God's glory from manifesting in my life, be paralysed, in the name of Jesus.

I loose myself from the spirit of desolation, in the name of Jesus.

Father Lord break me through in my home, in the name of Jesus.

Father Lord keep in me healthy, in the name of Jesus.

Father Lord break me through in my business, in the name of Jesus.

Let God be God in my economy, in the name of Jesus.

Glory of God, envelope every department of my life, in the name of Jesus.

The Lord that answereth by fire, be my God, in the name of Jesus.

By the blood of Jesus, all my enemies shall scatter to rise no more, in the name of Jesus.

Blood of Jesus, cry against all evil gatherings arranged for my sake, in the name of Jesus.

Father Lord, convert all my past failures to unlimited victories, in the name of Jesus.

Lord Jesus, create room for my advancement in every area of my life.

All evil thoughts against me, Lord turn them to be good for me.

Father Lord, give evil men for my life where evil decisions have been taken against me, in the name of Jesus.

Father Lord, advertise Your dumbfounding prosperity in my life.

Let the showers of dumbfounding prosperity fall in every department of my life, in the name of Jesus.

By the blood of Jesus, I claim all my prosperity in the name of Jesus.

Every door of my prosperity that has been shut, be opened now, in the name of Jesus.

Father Lord, convert my poverty to prosperity, in the name of Jesus.

Father Lord, convert my mistake to perfection, in the name of Jesus.

Father Lord, convert my frustration to fulfillment, in the name of Jesus.

Father Lord, bring honey out of the rock for me, in the name of Jesus.

By the blood of Jesus, I stand against every evil covenant of sudden death, in the name of Jesus.

By the blood of Jesus, I break every conscious and unconscious evil covenant of untimely death, in the name of Jesus.

You spirit of death and hell, you have no document in my life, in the name of Jesus.

You stones of death, depart from my ways, in the name of Jesus.

Father Lord, make me a voice of deliverance and blessing.

By the blood of Jesus, I tread upon the high places of the enemies, in the name of Jesus.

I bind and render useless, every blood sucking demon, in the name of Jesus.

You evil current of death, loose your grip over my life, in the name of Jesus.

By the blood of Jesus, I frustrate the decisions of the evil openers in my family, in the name of Jesus.

Fire of protection, cover my family, in the name of Jesus.

Father Lord, make my way perfect, in the name of Jesus.

Throughout the days of my life, I shall not be put to shame, in the name of Jesus.

By the blood of Jesus, I reject every garment of shame, in the name of Jesus.

By the blood of Jesus, I reject every shoe of shame, in the name of Jesus.

By the blood of Jesus, I reject every head-gear and cap of shame, in the name of Jesus.

Shamefulness shall not be my lot, in the name of Jesus.

Every demonic limitation of my progress as a result of shame, be removed, in the name of Jesus.

Every network of shame around me, be paralysed, in the name of Jesus.

Those who seek for my shame shall die for my sake, in the name of Jesus.

As far as shame is concerned, I shall not record any point for satan, in the name of Jesus.

I shall not eat the bread sorrow, shame, and defeat in Jesus Name.

No evil will touch me throughout my life, in the name of Jesus.

By the blood of Jesus, In every area of my life, my enemies will not catch me, in the name of Jesus.

By the blood of Jesus, In every area of my life, I shall run and not grow weary, I shall walk and shall not faint.

Father Lord, in every area of my life, let not my life disgrace You.

By the blood of Jesus, I will not be a victim of failure and I shall not bite my finger for any reason, in the name of Jesus.

Holy Spirit of God, Help me O Lord, to meet up with God's standard for my life.

By the blood of Jesus, I refuse to be a candidate to the spirit of amputation, in the name of Jesus.

By the blood of Jesus, with each day of my life, I shall move to higher ground, in the name of Jesus.

Every spirit of shame set in motion against my life, I bind you, in the name of Jesus.

Every spirit competing with my breakthroughs, be chained, in the name of Jesus.

By the blood of Jesus, I bind every spirit of slavery , in the name of Jesus.

By the blood of Jesus, In every day of my life, I disgrace all my stubborn pursuers, in the name of Jesus.

By the blood of Jesus, I bind, every spirit of Herod, in the name of Jesus.

Every spirit challenging my God, be disgraced, in Jesus' name.

Every Red Sea before me, be parted, in the name of Jesus.

By the blood of Jesus, I command every spirit of bad ending to be bound in every area of my life, in the name of Jesus.

By the blood of Jesus, Every spirit of Saul, be disgraced in my life, in the name of Jesus.

By the blood of Jesus, Every spirit of Pharaoh, be disgraced in my life, in Jesus' name.

By the blood of Jesus, I reject every evil invitation to backwardness, in Jesus' name.

By the blood of Jesus, I command every stone of hindrance in my life to be rolled away, in the name of Jesus.

Father Lord, roll away every stone of poverty from my life, in the name Jesus.

Let every stone of infertility in my marriage be rolled away, in the name of Jesus.

Let every stone of non-achievement in my life be rolled away, in the name of Jesus.

My God, roll away every stone of hardship and slavery from my life, in the name of Jesus.

My God, roll away every stone of failure planted in my life, my home and in my business, in the name of Jesus.

You stones of hindrance, planted at the edge of my breakthroughs, be rolled away, in the name of Jesus.

You stones of stagnancy, stationed at the border of my life, be rolled away, in the name of Jesus.

Father Lord, I thank You for all the stones You have rolled away, I forbid their return, in the name of Jesus.

Let the power from above come upon me, in the name of Jesus.

Father Lord, advertise Your power in every area of my life.

Father Lord, make me a power generator, throughout the days of my life, in the name of Jesus.

Let the power to live a holy life throughout the days of my life fall upon me, in the name of Jesus.

Let the power to live a victorious life throughout the days of my life fall upon me, in the name of Jesus.

Let the power to prosper throughout the days of my life fall upon me, in the name of Jesus.

Let the power to be in good health throughout the days of my life fall upon me, in the name of Jesus.

Let the power to disgrace my enemies throughout the days of my life fall upon me, in the name of Jesus.

Let the power of Christ rest upon me now, in the name of Jesus.

Let the power to bind and loose fall upon me now, in the name of Jesus.

Father Lord, let Your key of revival unlock every department of my life for Your revival fire, in the name of Jesus.

Every area of my life that is at the point of death, receive the touch of revival, in the name of Jesus.

Father Lord, send down Your fire and anointing into my life, in the name of Jesus.

Every uncrucified area in my life, receive the touch of fire and be crucified, in the name of Jesus.

Let the fire fall and consume all hindrances to my advancement, in the name of Jesus.

You stubborn problems in my life, receive the Holy Ghost dynamite, in the name of Jesus.

You carry-over miracle from my past, receive the touch of fire in the name of Jesus.

Holy Ghost fire, baptize me with prayer miracle, in Jesus' name.

By the blood of Jesus, Every area of my life that needs deliverance, receive the touch of fire and be delivered, in the name of Jesus.

Let my angels of blessing locate me now, in the name of Jesus.

Every satanic programme of impossibility, I cancel you now, in the name of Jesus.

Every household wickedness and its programme of impossibility, be paralysed, in the name of Jesus.

No curse will land on my head, in the name of Jesus.

Throughout the days of my life, I will not waste money on my health: the Lord shall be my healer, in the name of Jesus.

Throughout the days of my life, I will be in the right place at the right time.

Throughout the days of my life, I will not depart from the fire of God's protection, in the name of Jesus.

Throughout the days of my life, I will not be a candidate for incurable disease, in the name of Jesus.

Every weapon of captivity, be disgraced, in the name of Jesus.

Let every attack planned against the progress of my life be frustrated, in the name of Jesus.

I command the spirits of harassment and torment to leave me, in the name of Jesus.

Lord, begin to speak soundness into my mind and being.

I reverse every witchcraft curse issued against my progress.

I condemn all the spirits condemning me, in the name of Jesus.

Let divine accuracy come into my life and operations, in the name of Jesus.

No evil directive will manifest in my life, in the name of Jesus.

Let the plans and purposes of heaven be fulfilled in my life, in the name of Jesus.

O Lord, bring to me friends that reverence Your name and keep all others away.

Let divine strength come into my life, in the name of Jesus.

Let every stronghold working against my peace be destroyed, in the name of Jesus.

Let the power to destroy every decree of darkness operating in my life fall upon me now, in the name of Jesus.

Lord, deliver my tongue from evil silence.

Lord, let my tongue tell others of Your life.

Lord, loose my tongue and use it for Your glory.

Lord, let my tongue bring straying sheep back to the fold.

Lord, let my tongue strengthen those who are discouraged.

Lord, let my tongue guide the sad and the lonely.

Lord, baptise my tongue with love and fire.

Let every unrepentant and stubborn pursuers be disgraced in my life, in the name of Jesus.

Let every iron-like curse working against my life be broken by the blood of Jesus, in the name of Jesus.

Let every problem designed to disgrace me receive open shame, in the name of Jesus.

Let every problem anchor in my life be uprooted, in Jesus' name.

Multiple evil covenants, be broken by the blood of Jesus, in the name of Jesus.

Multiple curses, be broken by the blood of Jesus, in Jesus' name.

Everything done against me with evil padlocks, be nullified by the blood of Jesus, in the name of Jesus.

Everything done against me at any cross-roads, be nullified by the blood of Jesus, in the name of Jesus.

Chapter 2   The Reward of Hope In God

Let every stubborn and prayer resisting demon receive stones of fire and thunder, in the name of Jesus.

Every stubborn and prayer resisting sickness, loose your evil hold upon my life, in the name of Jesus.

Every problem associated with the dead, be smashed by the blood of Jesus, in the name of Jesus.

I recover my stolen property seven fold, in the name of Jesus.

Let every evil memory about me be erased by the blood of Jesus, in the name of Jesus.

By the blood of Jesus, I disallow my breakthroughs from being caged, in Jesus' name.

Let the sun of my prosperity arise and scatter every cloud of poverty, in the name of Jesus.

I decree unstoppable advancement upon my life, in Jesus' name.

I soak every day of my life in the blood of Jesus and in signs and wonders, in the name of Jesus.

I break every stronghold of oppression in my life.

Let every satanic joy about my life be terminated, in the name of Jesus.

I paralyze every household wickedness, in the name of Jesus.

Let every satanic spreading river dry up by the blood of Jesus, in the name of Jesus.

I bind every ancestral spirit and command them to loose their hold over my life, in the name of Jesus.

CONCLUSION

"For there is hope of a tree, if it be cut down, that it will sprout again, and that the tender branch thereof will not cease.."
(Job 14:7)

Among my primary reason to write this small book is to reassure you that there is hope for you in God. I do not know the details of your story but I do know that *there is hope for you in God.*

"Let us hear the conclusion of the whole matter: Fear God, and keep his commandments: for this is the whole duty of man.For God shall bring every work into judgment, with every secret thing, whether it be good, or whether it be evil." **(Eccl 12:13-14)**

In this physical realm, *"there is hope for you."* Never quit because you are facing prevailing circumstance. Never quite because you do not have a job. Never quit because you failed the last time you tried. I like to reaffirm to you that God have a plan for you, a plan of good, and not evil, to give you a future and an unexpected end. It is my heart desire that you make plans for eternity. Remember, *winners never quit and those who quit never win in life.*

If you are a born again Christian; we like to encourage you in your Christian life. If you are not a born again Christian we can help you here receive genuine salvation. *"Therefore if any man be in Christ, he is a new creature: old things are passed away; behold, all things are become new."* (2 Cor 5:17)

Now repeat this Prayer after me

Say Lord Jesus, I accept you today, as my Lord and my savior, forgive me of my sins wash me with your blood. Right now, I believe, I am sanctified, I am save, I am free, I am free from the Power of sin to serve the Lord Jesus. Thank you Lord for saving me. Amen.

Congratulations: You are now...

A BORN AGAIN CHRISTIAN.

Again I say to you—

CONGRATULATIONS!

What must I do to determine my divine visitation?

To determine divine visitation you must be born again! The word says, *"As many as received him, to them gave He power to become the sons of God. Even to them that believe on his name."* (John 1:12)

To qualify for divine visitation, do the following with sincerity—

1) Acknowledge that you are a sinner and that He died for you. (Romans 3:23)

2) Repent of your sins. (Acts 3:19, Luke 13:5, 2 Peter 3:9)

3) Believe in your heart that Jesus died for your sin. (Romans 10:10)

4) Confess Jesus as the Lord over your life. (Romans 10:10, Acts 2:21)

"Therefore if any man be in Christ, he is a new creature: old things are passed away; behold, all things are become new." (2 Cor 5:17)

Now repeat this Prayer after me

Say Lord Jesus, I accept you today, as my Lord and my savior, forgive me of my sins wash me with your blood. Right now, I believe, I am sanctified, I am save, I am free, I am free from the Power of sin to serve the Lord Jesus. Thank you Lord for saving me. Amen.

Congratulations: You are now...

A BORN AGAIN CHRISTIAN.

Again I say to you—

CONGRATULATIONS!

I guarantee you! Watch the Spirit of God bear witness with your Spirit confirming His word with signs following. The word says, *"The Spirit itself beareth witness with our spirit, that we are the children of God."* (Romans 8:16)

Join a bible believing church or join us on our weekly and Sunday worship services at 343 Sanford Avenue, Newark, New Jersey 07106.

WISDOM KEYS

— Every Productive Society is a society heading to the top.

— Millions of Nigerians run away from Nigeria, very few Nigerians stay in Nigeria.

— My decision to return Nigeria is the will of God for my life.

— My short coming in America after 18 years, trained me to be wise, to think, reflect and reason appropriately.

— If you train your mind to reason it will train your hands to earn money.

— It is absurd to use the money of the heathen to build the kingdom of the living God.

— Every Ministry reveals its agenda and goal either at the beginning or at the end. Be careful of your life it is your first Ministry.

— The average American mind is conditioned for a continual quest to get new things and (discard the former) and throw away old things.

— When I considered well, my BMW jeep became my initial deposit for the work of the ministry in Nigeria.

— Money will never fall from any tree.

— Everyone is waiting for you to change your mind until you change your thinking nothing changes around you.

— Multiple academic degrees in other discipline gave me the chance to think, reflect and reason

— What so everyone are thinking and reflecting at the moment reveals you to the time and the now factor

— All events and intents are the product of precise thought processes, accurate reason every event is designed for a designated timeline

— Wisdom is your ability to think, to create and invent. If you can think wise enough you will come out of penury

— The distance between you and success is your creative ability to think reason and reflect accurate.

— Success is the result of hard work, commitment resolve and determination learning from past mistakes and failing.

— If you organize your mind you have organized your life and destiny.

— There is a thin line between success and failure. If you look above and beyond you are on your way to success.

— Wealth is your ability to think, power is your ability to reason and success is your ability to be informed.

— If you can make use of your mind by thinking and reasoning God will make use of your life and destiny.

— Think and Be Great.

— Reflect, Reason, think and be great.

— Famous people are born of woman

— That you will make it is your intention; that you will survive is your resolve, that you will succeed with changes is your determination, personal efforts and hard work.

— No man was born a failure. Lack of vision is the end product of failure.

— Working with mental patients encourages and aspire me to be a productive observant and dedicated to my assignment.

— Successful people are not magicians, it is the will power combined with hard work, and determination and a resolve to succeed that make them succeed.

— In the unequivocal state of the mind, intention is not a location or a position it is the state of the mind.

— So many people think, that they think. The mind is used to think, reflect, and reason. You will remain blind with your eye open until you can see with your mind by thinking.

— There is no favoritism in accurate and precise calculation.

— Although knowledge is power, information is the key and gateway to a great future.

— It will take the hand of God to move the hand of man.

— With the backing of the great wise God, nothing will disconnect you from your inheritance.

— As long as you have wisdom and understanding of God, Satan and evil cannot manipulate your life and destiny.

— You have come this far by yourself judgment and decision you have made in the past, now lean and listen to God for another dimension of greatness.

— Great people are common people it is extra ordinary effort and the price of sacrifice that produces greatness.

— As a mental direct care worker I saw a great pastor and a motivational speaker within myself.

— Menial job does not reduce your self-worth, until you resolve to achieve greatness see greatness in all you do; you will never count in your community.

— The principle of Jesus will solve your gambling and addiction problems

— The man of Jesus will lead you into heaven,

— Everyone have their self-appraisal and what they think about you. Until you discover yourself other opinion about you will alter the real you.

— Supervisors and directors are just a position in the chain of command in a work place. Never allow your supervisor hierarchy to alter your opinion about yourself.

— Everyone can come out of debt if they make up their mind.

— That I am not a decision maker at work does not diminish my contribution to my world.

— Although it appears like it was a poor decision to accept a direct care employment at a psychiatric hospital as I reflect of my nine years of experience, it became apparent that I have learnt and experienced enough for my next assignment in life.

— Self-encouragement and determination is a resolve of the heart.

— If you are determined to make a difference, and do the things that make a difference you will eventually make a difference.

— Good things do not come easy

— Short cuts will cut your life short.

— Those who look ahead move ahead.

— Life is all about making an impact. In your life time strive to make an impact in your community.

— Make friends and connect with people who are moving ahead of you in life.

— If you can look around well you have come a long way in your life, made a lot of difference and realized a lot of success in life.

— If you are my old friend, hurry up to reach out to me before I become a stranger to you.

— Everything I am blessed with inspirations from God, that change my definition and interpretation of the world around me.

— I thought I was stagnant and lonely until I looked around and noticed my children running around and my wife cooking.

— At 40 I resigned my Job to seek the Lord forever.

— My ministry took a drastic rise to the top when the wisdom of God visited me with knowledge and understanding.

— You will be a better person, if you understand the characteristics of your personality – your mood swings, attitudes, and habits.

— It is the seed of love you sow into the heart of a child and a woman that you reap in due time.

— Love is not selfish, love share everything including the concealed secrets of the mind.

— As long as you have a prayer life and a bible; you will never feel lonely, rejected, and idle in the race of life.

— When good friends disconnect from you, let them go, they might have seen something new in a different direction.

— Confidence in yourself and in God is the only way to bring you out of captivity.

— Never train a child to waste his/her time.

— The mind is the greatest assets of a great future.

— You walk by common sense run by principles and fly by instruction.

— Those who fly in flight of life fly alone.

— Up in the air you are alone. No one can toll you accept the compass of knowledge and information.

— I have seen a towing vehicle I have seen a towing ship I have never seen a tolling airplane.

— I exercise my judgment and make a decision every minute of the day.

— Decisions are crucial, critical and vital with reference to your future.

— So many people wish for a great future. You can only work towards a great future.

— Your celebrity status began when you discovered your talent. What are you good at? Work at it with all commitment.

— Prayers will sustain you but the wisdom of God will prosper you.

— When I met Oyedepo, his teachings changed my perspective. But when I met Ibiyeomie; His teaching changed my perception.

— I will be successful in ministry if only I concentrate and focus my energy in the work of the ministry.

— It took the late Dr. Vincent Pearle Norman's book to open my mind towards kingdom success.

CHAPTER 3

PRAYER OF SALVATION

"Neither is there salvation in any other: for there is none other name under heaven given among men, whereby we must be saved."
Acts 4:12

What must I do to determine my salvation?

To be saved we must be born again! The word says as many as received him, to them gave He power to become the sons of God. Even to them that believe on his name.

To qualify for divine visitation, do the following with sincerity—

1) Acknowledge that you are a sinner and that He died for you. (Romans 3:23)

2) Repent of your sins. (Acts 3:19, Luke 13:5, 2 Peter 3:9)

3) Believe in your heart that Jesus died for your sin. (Romans 10:10)

Chapter 3 — Prayer of Salvation

4) Confess Jesus as the Lord over your life. (Romans 10:10, Acts 2:21)

Now repeat this Prayer after me

Say Lord Jesus, I accept you today, as my Lord and my savior, forgive me of my sins wash me with your blood. Right now, I believe, I am sanctified, I am save, I am free, I am free from the Power of sin to serve the Lord Jesus. Thank you Lord for saving me. Amen.

Congratulations: You are now...

A BORN AGAIN CHRISTIAN.

Again I say to you—

CONGRATULATIONS!

I adjure you to watch the Spirit of God bear witness with your Spirit confirming His word with signs following. The word says The Spirit itself beareth witness with our spirit, that we are the children of God.

MIRACLE CARE OUTREACH

*"...But that the members should have
the same care one for another"*
1 Corinthians 12:25

    We are all members of the body of Christ. Jesus commanded us to love our neighbor as ourselves. This includes caring for one another as a member of one body. True love is expressed in caring and giving. The word says for God so Love He gave....

    Reach out to someone in need of Jesus, help someone in crisis find Christ. Look out and prove your love to Jesus by caring and inviting your friends and associates to find Jesus the Healer.

    Invite your friends to our Home Care Cell Fellowship (Miracle chapel Intl Satellite fellowship) In the USA at 33 Schley Street Newark New Jersey 07112. Home Care Cell fellowship Group meets every Tuesday at 6:00pm-7:00pm.

    If you are in Nigeria—**MIRACLE OF GOD MINISTRIES**, aka **"MIRACLE CHAPEL INTL"** Mpama –Egbu-Owerri Imo state Nigeria.

LIFE IS NOT ALL ABOUT DURATION— BUT ITS ALL ABOUT DONATION

What does the above statement mean?....

Life consists not in accumulation of material wealth. (Luke 12:15) But it's all about liberality...i.e., what you can give and share with others. (Proverbs 11:25) When you live for others, you live forever—because you out-live your generation by the legacy you live behind after you depart into glory to be with the Lord. But when you live to yourself, when you are reduced to SELF—you are easily forgotten when you die and depart in glory.

Permit me to admonish you today to live your life to be a blessing to a soul connected to you today. I want you to know that so many souls are connected and looking up to you, and through you so many souls will be saved and rescued from destruction. Will you disciple someone today to find Jesus Christ?

As a genuine Christian; it is your duty to evangelize Jesus Christ to all you meet on your way. Jesus is still in the healing business—Jesus is still doing miracles from time of old to now. Therefore, tell someone about Jesus Christ today, disciple and bring them to Church. *Philip findeth Nathanael...* (John 1:45)

Please to prove the sincerity of your love for God today; please become a soul winner. The dignity of your Christianity is hidden in your boldness to proclaim and evangelize Jesus Christ to all you meet on your way. There is a question mark on the integrity of your Christianity until you become a life soul winner. Invite someone to join us worship the Lord Jesus this coming Sunday. Amen

Chapter 3   Prayer of Salvation

MIRACLE OF GOD MINISTRIES

PILLARS OF THE COMMISSION

We Believe Preach and Practice the following:

1) We believe and preach Salvation to every living human being

2) We believe and preach Repentance and forgiveness of sins

3) We believe and preach the baptism of the Holy Spirit and Spiritual gifts

4) We believe and teach the Prosperity

5) We believe and preach Divine Healing and Miracles (Signs &Wonder)

6) We believe and preach Faith

7) We believe and proclaim the Power of God (Supernatural)

8) We believe and proclaim Praise& Worship to God

9) We believe and preach Wisdom

10) We believe and preach Holiness (Consecration)

11) We believe and preach Vision

12) We believe and teach the Word of God

13) We believe and teach Success

14) We believe and practice Prayer

15) We believe and teach Deliverance

These 15 stones form the Pillars of Our Commission. Become part of this church family and follow this great move of God.

MY HEART FELT PRAYER FOR YOU

It is my prayer that you testify today about the goodness of the Lord. I desire for you to have an encounter with our Lord Jesus Christ.

Now let me Pray for you:

Heavenly father I thank you for this great opportunity of prayer, even as I pray and prophesy over this precious one reading this book. May this day, be a day of encounter with your Spirit. May they experience you in a new dimension of a higher order. May today be a day of encounter with the supernatural for them. Lord do that which no man can do for them and take all the glory. In Jesus Mighty Name. Amen. We thank you Jesus for hearing us. In Jesus mighty name. Amen.

TIME TO SEEK THE FACE OF THE LORD IN PRAYERS

Often we fail to seek the face of the Lord in prayer and in the word of God. We must remember that the more we know him the more He will reveal himself to us. We are told that God is not partial. Whatever He did for one, He will do for all in life. It is written *"Then Peter opened his mouth, and said, Of a truth I perceive that God is no respecter of persons"* (Acts 10:34) We are told *"For there is no respect of persons with God."* (Romans 2:11)

We must always seek the face of the Lord in prayer, in intercession and in thanksgiving. Anyone without a prayer life has no value to meet with God. We encounter God in prayers. Every time we pray we meet with God. I will encourage you to continue seeking the face of the Lord in prayers, in thanksgiving and in intercession. Prayer is so important to the Lord Jesus that He taught His apostles how to pray.

"And it came to pass, that, as he was praying in a certain place, when he ceased, one of his disciples said unto him, Lord, teach us to pray, as John also taught his disciples.

And he said unto them, When ye pray, say, Our Father which art in heaven, Hallowed be thy name. Thy kingdom come. Thy will be done, as in heaven, so in earth.

Give us day by day our daily bread.

And forgive us our sins; for we also forgive every one that is indebted to us. And lead us not into temptation; but deliver us from evil."

(Luke 11:1-4). I pray you embrace prayer as a lifestyle into you own life.

CHAPTER 4

ABOUT THE AUTHOR

Rev Franklin N Abazie is the founding and Presiding Pastor of Miracle of God Ministries with headquarters in Newark, New Jersey USA and a branch church in Owerri- Imo State Nigeria. He is following the footsteps of one of his mentors, Oral Roberts (Healing Evangelist) of the blessed memory. The Lord passed Oral Roberts healing mantle two days before he went to be with the Lord at age 91 into the hand of healing evangelist-Rev Franklin N Abazie in a vision.

In all his services the Power and Presence of God is present to heal all in his audience. He is an ordained man of God with a Healing Ministry reviving the healing and miracle ministry of Jesus Christ of Nazareth.

Pastor Franklin N Abazie, is called by God with a unique mandate: **"THE MOMENT IS DUE TO IMPACT YOUR WORLD THROUGH THE REVIVAL OF THE HEALING & MIRACLE MINISTRY OF JESUS CHRIST OF NAZARETH**

"I AM SENDING YOU TO RESTORE HEALTH UNTO THEE AND I WILL HEAL THEE OF THY WOUNDS. SAID THE LORD OF HOST"

Rev. Abazie is a gifted ardent Teacher of the word of God who operates also in the office of a Prophet, generating and attracting undeniable signs & wonders, special miracles and healings, with apostolic fireworks of the Holy Ghost. He is the founding and presiding senior Pastor of this fast growing Healing ministry. He has written over **86** inspirational, healing and transforming books covering almost all aspect of divine healing and life. He is happily married and blessed with children.

BOOKS BY REV FRANKLIN N ABAZIE

1) The Outcome of Faith
2) Understanding the secret of prevailing Prayers
3) Commanding Abundance
4) Understanding the secret of the man God uses
5) Activating my due Season
6) Overcoming Divine Verdicts
7) The Outcome of Divine Wisdom
8) Understanding God's Restoration Mandate
9) Walking in the Victory and Authority of the truth
10) Gods Covenant Exemption
11) Destiny Restoration Pillars
12) Provoking Acceptable Praise
13) Understanding Divine Judgment
14) Activating Angelic Re-enforcement
15) Provoking Un-Merited Favor
16) The Benefits of the Speaking faith
17) Understanding Divine Arrangement
18) Put your faith to work
19) Developing a positive attitude in life
20) The Power of Prevailing faith
21) Inexplicable faith
22) The intellectual components of Redemption.
23) Dominating Controlling Spirit
24) Understanding Divine Prosperity
25) Understanding the secret of the man God Uses
26) Retaining Your Inheritance
27) Never give up hope
28) Commanding Angelic Escorts
29) The winner's faith
30) Understanding Your Guardian Angels
31) Overcoming the Dominion of Sin
32) Understanding the Voice of God
33) The Outstanding benefits of the Anointing

34) The Audacity of the Blood of Jesus
35) Walking in the Reality of the Anointing
36) The Mystery of Divine supply
37) Understanding Your Harvest Season
38) Activating Your Success Buttons
39) Overcoming the forces of Darkness
40) Overcoming the devices of the devil
41) Overcoming Demonic agents
42) Overcoming the sorrows of failure
43) Rejecting the Sorrows of failure
44) Resisting the Sorrows of Poverty
45) The Restoring broken Marriages.
46) Redeeming Your Days
47) The force of Vision
48) Overcoming the forces of ignorance
49) Understanding the sacrifice of small beginning
50) The might of small beginning
51) Praying in the Spirit
52) Dominating controlling Spirits
53) Breaking the shackles of the curse of the law
54) Covenant keys to answered prayers
55) Wisdom for Signs & Wonders
56) Wisdom for generational Impact
57) Wisdom for Marriage Stability
58) Understanding the number of your Days
59) Enforcing Your Kingdom Rights
60) Escaping the traps of immoralities
61) Escaping the trap of Poverty
62) Accessing Biblical Prosperity
63) Accessing True Riches in Christ
64) Silencing the Voice of the Accuser
65) Overcoming the forces of oppositions
66) Quenching the voice of the avenger
67) Silencing demonic Prediction & Projection
68) Silencing Your Mocker
69) Understanding the Power of the Holy Ghost

Chapter 4   About The Author

70) Understanding the baptism of Power
71) The Mystery of the Blood of Jesus
72) Understanding the Mystery of Sanctification
73) Understanding the Power of Holiness
74) Praying in the spirit
75) Activating the Forces of Vengeance
76) Appreciating the Mystery of Restoration
77) Covenant Keys to Answered Prayers
78) Engaging the mystery of the blood
79) Commanding the Power of the Speaking faith
80) Uprooting the forces against Your Rising
81) Overcoming mere success syndrome
82) Understanding Divine Sentence
83) Understanding the Mystery of Praise
84) Understanding the Author of Faith
85) The Mystery of the finisher of faith
86) Where is your trust?

MIRACLE OF GOD MINISTRIES

NIGERIA CRUSADE
2012

www.ingramcontent.com/pod-product-compliance
Lightning Source LLC
Chambersburg PA
CBHW021444080526
44588CB00009B/688